ADVANCED
SQUASH

ADVANCED SQUASH

Jahangir Khan

with Rahmat Khan and Richard Eaton

Stanley Paul

LONDON · SYDNEY · AUCKLAND · JOHANNESBURG

By the same authors:

Winning Squash (Stanley Paul, 1985)

Stanley Paul & Co. Ltd
An imprint of Random Century Group
20 Vauxhall Bridge Road, London SW1V 2SA

Random Century Australia (Pty) Ltd
20 Alfred Street, Milsons Point, Sydney 2061

Random Century New Zealand Limited
PO Box 40-086, Glenfield, Auckland 10

Random Century South Africa (Pty) Ltd
PO Box 337, Bergvlei 2012, South Africa

First published 1990

© Jahangir Khan and Rahmat Khan 1990

Set in Linotronic 300 Melior
Printed and bound in Great Britain by Scotprint
Ltd, Musselburgh, Scotland

British Library Cataloguing in Publication Data
Khan, Jahangir
    Advanced squash.
    1. Squash rackets.
    I. Title   II. Khan, Rahmat   III. Eaton, Richard
    796.343

ISBN 0 09 173692 7

Frontispiece: Jahangir Khan, poised, prepared and balanced for a forehand kill

Contents

Introduction   7

SECTION I – **Five Advances**

1. Discipline   9

2. Deception   18

3. Hitting Harder   30

4. Movement   47

5. Pressure   58

SECTION II – **Brushing up Basics**

6. The Drive   67

7. The Volley   74

8. The Short Game   81

SECTION III – **Planning the Future**

9. Playing for Life   86

Acknowledgements

Thanks are due to Roddy Bloomfield for providing the concept of this book, and to him and Dominique Shead for their encouragement to complete it; to Mary Eaton, for preparing, typing, and improving the manuscript; to Anne Lee for constant assistance; to Josie Khan for hospitality; and to squash players all over the world whose ability and personality has been an inspiration.

Photo acknowledgement
The publishers and authors would particularly like to thank Stephen Line, who provided all the photographs in this book except for those which are individually credited.

Introduction

So many people play squash these days. The professional circuit has spread to every continent on the globe, and about 15 million enjoy the game worldwide. The top men have won prizes everywhere – including pewter pots in Malaysia, diamond-studded balls in Antwerp, and gold rings in Toronto. The rank and file everywhere have earned themselves health, happiness, friends and fun. Inevitably many of them have become very good at the game.

Hence the need for a book to take beginners on to a more advanced standard, without intimidating them with large numbers of training routines that will diminish their motivation. If routines are what you need, 50 of them have been attractively shown in the Khan training tape, presented by Virgin video. If you need a refresher course before starting this book, try *Winning Squash* by the same authors.

By trying to push yourself to a higher standard you do not have to lose the fun of the game. Rather the reverse. Because squash is so accessible and sociable, it can be fitted into a busy schedule and combined with other leisure pursuits. And by investing more thought and effort, the gains in satisfaction are usually correspondingly greater.

An increasingly large minority have the opportunity to become serious part-time competitors or even full-time players trying to make the grade. This is particularly the case in England and Wales, where the development of a national league has linked the apex of world stars with leagues right down to the base of the pyramid. Many of these leagues offer the chance of financial rewards, and some enterprising players are able to acquire sponsorship as well.

Most important of all, there is an organic link from the grass roots to the top of the tree. We hope we can help you climb it.

RICHARD EATON

SECTION I – Five Advances
1. Discipline

2. Amanat Khan, the young hopeful.

The son of Torsam and nephew of Jahangir, Amanat is the latest to be burdened with having to live up to the most famous family name in squash. He still has a long way to go. But one quality in particular makes it possible that he can succeed – his discipline. If Amanat is required to be in bed by 9 p.m. he is there; and if he has to get up at 6 a.m. to do his training he does it. At the age of 17 he decided to make squash his life and after two years of work he was already getting on court with players he had only previously dreamed about. If he succeeds it will be another chapter in a fairytale. Amanat lost his father when he was very young and left Pakistan to live in England with Rahmat when he was 16. If he manages to follow in Jahangir's lofty footprints he will be the third generation of the family to make his name at the game. First Roshan Khan, British Open Champion in 1957, then Jahangir Khan, and now, perhaps, Amanat Khan?

Discipline

The universe, we think, has a natural order. Human beings in their daily lives do not. They must create it. If they do, they are capable of remarkable achievements. If they don't, they deteriorate. This has been proved in every walk of life – in industry and agriculture, in culture and the arts, in leisure and sport. An ordered existence is the forge of civilization. And the driving force of an ordered existence is discipline.

There has hardly been a leading squash player who has not possessed discipline. This is not something to be feared. Discipline should not be self-abasement, misery, somebody standing over you cracking a whip. It should be a framework, a plan, and a regimen. The framework creates goals, the plan provides the means of reaching them, and the regimen converts talent into achievement. Discipline is not negative, nor denial, but progressive, a method of self-realization.

You soon realize this if you are a squash coach. A high percentage of people come with problems that have to be tackled before progress can begin. Physical problems, mental problems, emotional problems – it is like disentangling a thicketed wood in order to allow growth.

Discipline for squash players involves the ability to turn up on time, to do training to the limit of their energy, and to be honest about what they fail to do. It also refers much more broadly to living in general. Squash should not be regarded as detached from day-to-day life. General conduct and attitudes have a direct bearing on both.

To be successful as an advanced player therefore requires an almost total approach. But people differ a great deal; personalities are diverse. Some need a rigid discipline whilst others are suffocated by it. They may need a gentler regime allowing expression, provided they do not lose sight of the goal. Discipline does not mean being inflexible. It should relate to your state at any particular time. When a player has had a very tough time the day before he may feel that he still has to get up early to go for a run. However, whilst this may be good for maintaining mental discipline, it may not be good for the body. So instead of a 6.00 a.m. start, it may have to be 10.00 a.m. A balance between the mental and physical has to be kept.

Crucial for good discipline is not to waste time. Keep a diary. When players are training it is best for them to write down what they have done. This encourages a sense of responsibility and can raise morale. Months later when players look back they can be surprised by how much they have done. It will reinforce the importance of keeping going till, bit by bit, a mountain is climbed. Such a diary will also show failures, and learning from these may be the most important thing of all.

The mind can often drag the body through, and although you should not rely on that, you want to retain the ability to do this in a match. Hence rigid adherence to an early start can be a danger. One or two players have created health problems for themselves in this way. They press on with their routine even when they are tired. Then they find they cannot sleep. When they come on to court, they have no ball control, and can't control their temper. They fight with their wives or husbands for no reason and

3. *Discipline involves turning up on time and being honest about what you fail to do. It also involves meticulously performing warming-up and stretching exercises, as Jahangir does here*

eventually find that they have nothing left.

One famous player went on holiday with his wife on the strict agreement that he would do no training. He kept it up for two days. On the third day he sneaked out, early. His wife woke up and he wasn't there. Another fight followed. In the end his wife had to compromise. It's no good letting guilt feelings about breaking a regime build up to an obsession like it did for that player.

The secret of discipline, therefore, is balance. Balance between rest, playing, running, exercises, court training, and ball control. Don't forget ball control. Many players go and play and overlook all the little practices that are

so important. Even if it is only half an hour or 15 minutes, still do it. If you have an evening match, go and hit the ball in the morning; it will take a lot of pressure off you.

The night's sleep is crucial for good discipline the next day. Early to bed, early to sleep, early to rise – these create a feeling you can only understand by experiencing it. Go out into the garden early, winter or summer, and think about your life and your surroundings. You will experience a kind of energy in your mind and in your body. You become aware of your ambition and what it is all about. You may feel a great desire to pursue it with all your heart. Arising early, well rested in mind and body, creates a new-born feeling, full of new life.

A full-time squash player should start running in the morning, and continue through the day in three sessions. It is sometimes boring and painful, but this is the groundwork that builds up basic strength. After the background running he or she can move on to court exercises, and quicker work, such as 400 metres. One lap of a track, repeated often with only 30 second intervals, will really develop your speed.

Never start the day (or a training programme) with sprints. Begin with a long jog, which is good for the whole body. Develop speed work closer to tournament time. Speed work takes a lot more out of the body and is often better done over a short period of time.

There has, however, been a change of ideas recently, and some players do speed work over a longer period. They do a long jog one day and sprints the next. If this is what you prefer, it might be better to vary the sprints – e.g. jog, then run 400 metres; jog, 200; jog, 400; etcetera. Though if you can do the 400 metres properly once a week, with the right times, that is really all you need.

When following a training programme, honesty is essential. Some players lie to themselves and to their coaches about what they have done. It seems amazing but it happens, and quite often. The reason for it is pride. Players want to cover up their inability to do something. But if they do, the inability will remain. A coach and a player can never work like this. If a coach finds out about the lie he is likely to call it quits.

Players can declare themselves ready to do anything to achieve their ambition, but when it comes to it succumb to distractions and temptations. Learn for yourself what your priorities are, and the importance of being honest about them. This can raise wider issues: what is this life all about? We're here but we've often forgotten why.

It can be helpful to investigate things this deeply, to dig up the fuel for real ambition. Success at a high level in squash may mean acquiring self-knowledge and developing habits that create solid character. Heavy though this may sound, it can be preferable to operating with a mind cluttered by things that mean little, leaving less room for squash. Players inevitably get depressed and tired, and rather than turn to false remedies, it may be better to have a heart to heart with a coach or a helper they trust.

This is frequently the first thing a player has to realize. Some scorn it, but adopting a broad spiritual or philosophical approach can make the difference between success and failure. It helps you adopt the right attitudes to success and failure. Whilst you are improving, failure may be the thing you experience most. So it is important to build up inner strength, to be prepared for such set-backs. Without this determination you get nowhere. With it, a tranformation can gradually take place.

This is because every loss provides potential gain – particularly in knowledge as to what happened and why. But to realize this potential requires a profounder perspective. The ability to see that losing a squash match is just a small part of something much bigger helps give you the energy to recover.

However, there comes a time when a player cannot be expected to take any more. That is when he or she needs to be told not to worry about winning or losing, but only about giving 100 per cent. This can relieve the pressure. Similarly, when a player has come out of the court during a match, having just lost a game, there should be no recrimination. That requires discipline from the coach as well.

Many obstacles lie in the path of a player striving to give 100 per cent. You would hardly believe how trivial some of them seem, but trivial they are not. Stray remarks from outsiders before a match impinge themselves on the mind. Negative thoughts of a thousand kinds develop. An outstanding way to fight against this is to prepare thoroughly. Many times I escaped from trouble in a match after Rahmat requested, 'Show me again what you have done in training.'

Discipline in training is therefore crucial. Perform the routines according to rules, and if necessary award points for success and failure. Too much training is done without the framework of rules, and then in the totally different situation of a match the pressure becomes too great. This controlled training must be done

4. *Do the routines according to the rules. For much of his career Jahangir trained with the help of Rahmat Khan, here seen creating the framework for the discipline*

every day, so that miracles are not expected in a match.

Players sometimes give less than 100 per cent because they feel they are playing badly. This is an illogical reaction − exactly the reverse of what should occur − but it often happens. Therefore a disciplined pattern of how to use your strokes is needed. The Jahangir Khan videotape describes 50 different routines to help develop such techniques. Follow the routines with no mistakes, no hitting the tin. Then you will have the knowledge and ability to put things right when not playing well.

It is said that the mark of a champion is if he can win while not playing well. It is also the mark of a hard worker, who labours every day, regardless of whether he feels like it or not. This is where a trainer is so valuable: he can remind you of what you are trying to do; and help on those off-days when you don't realize you are not giving 100 per cent.

However, there are times when you really should take it easy. If an ailment is in the mind, it can often be cured with just two or three words. If it is a genuine sickness, take care, because that can destroy the body. Sometimes there is a fine line between sickness and health, but if you have 'flu training can be dangerous. Getting by on sheer will-power in a match is one thing, but using will-power alone in training is quite another. You may be laying up problems for later. Weigh your decision carefully.

Discipline extends to conduct on court. Make people laugh by all means. But if you cause distractions that put referees and opponents against you, it will do nobody any good in the long term. There is much more of this than there used to be, because there is more money, more competition, more pressure.

It is better not to argue with officials at all. You have the referee for better or worse. Whether he is good or bad − and we know referees don't always make good decisions − don't lose your temper with him. Question him, as pleasantly as you can, if you are really frustrated. If he explains, then the conversation should be finished.

Some players take the view that by putting the referee or marker under pressure, they will over a period of time get an extra point or two. It may only be a point a match, but by keeping on querying and arguing, it can make a difference. That view is wrong ethically, and practically too. It can just as often turn the referee against you and it can spoil your relationship with him both on and off the court. Then you end up playing against two people.

Cheating is to be avoided. The Jahangir philosophy has been as follows. Don't cheat, but if somebody cheats against you − let's say by picking up a double bounce and pretending it is all right − then occasionally you might do the same. This is competition and the referee should sort it out. Turning the other cheek simply puts you at a disadvantage. Some players will turn and hit you with the racket, so there may be nothing wrong if you do the same, to show that cheats will not prosper. But calculated cheating is quite wrong.

To repeat, discipline is a way of life. It is necessary in your everyday behaviour. You need discipline whether faced with a referee, or a sponsor, or a promoter. Many players do not do the right things on the squash circuit, and this puts people against them, creating more pressure than is already there. Such players may enter the court with a feeling of guilt. We want you to have a clear heart and mind.

5. *A trainer can be so valuable. Here Aman Khan, an outstanding trainer, helps England international Fiona Greaves (Fritz Borchert)*

Amanat Khan demonstrates a few exercises to help a player's performance:

A.
Discipline and how to begin it. Amanat Khan hits the road early in the day for his strength-developing run

B.
Discipline and how to continue it. Like many players Amanat finds skipping an excellent complement to running or jogging. It helps create the bouncy alertness necessary for the ready position on the 'T'

C. and D.
Warming up and warming down are crucial components of the disciplined player. It improves flexibility and helps avoid injury

E., F., G. and H.
Four studies in stretching. It takes mental discipline to perform these physical exercises by yourself. But they can reward you with the extra suppleness an advanced player needs to improve court-covering capacity

C

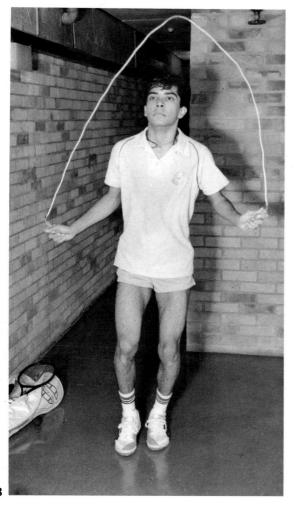

B

E

F

G

D

H

2. Deception

6. Qamar Zaman, the master of deception.

Zaman has been one of the most entertaining players there has ever been, not only because he is a funny man and a brilliant strokemaker, but because you never knew what he was going to do next. He was British Open Champion in 1975 and world number one in 1979, but perhaps the most remarkable fact about him was that he never won either of the world's two great titles after this one British Open triumph. However, between 1977 and 1984 he was runner-up in the World Open and British Open four times each, which gives an idea of how long he was at the forefront of the game. His deception was often created by a jerk in his swing which is probably inadvisable for budding young players to copy. But his flexible footwork and devious late movements of the wrist were an example of just how much damage could be created in opponents' defences, even at the very highest level, by imaginative use of creative skills.

Deception

Deception is the language of top squash. Without it your racket cannot be eloquent. Without it, your technique and your tactics become predictable, your style will become bland, and your opponent able to prevent you from implementing your skills. But with it, you command an audience. The opponent must watch, listen and try to anticipate what is coming next. That can be a difficult and tiresome business. He never has peace.

Deception is what makes a first-class player. It often characterizes him. It means to be creative and to develop one's own way of doing things. It means to be an individual. There are many different ways of being deceptive.

These days it is more important to mask the shot and bluff the opponent than ever before. An increasing number of players are fit enough to run all day. They will wear you down unless you jerk them around, make them move at the last second and take them the furthest possible distance to get to the ball.

Deception is valuable not only for taking openings and winning points. It has a longer term purpose than that. It can be used to make opponents expend the maximum energy with every rally and every stroke, draining their fuel tank and slowing their body's engine down.

When a player is able to employ this sort of deception, on a regular basis and without making mistakes, the whole game changes. Something simple becomes complex. Squash develops complications in stroke production, tactics and, inevitably, psychology as well. There becomes a limitless number of possibilities and surprises. This is not always obvious to the spectactor. It can be a subtle process.

Many people will watch a long rally and think it repetitive and attritional. Instead there is a discreet beauty, an intricate variety, and a jockeying for advantage that is both primitive and sophisticated.

Deception can be brought about by sleight of hand, wrist, arm, and even foot or body. By far the most frequent method is the late movement of the wrist, that can turn a straight drive into a cross-court, or pull it further across into a reverse angle, or fade it into a boast. Four shots all with the same preparation. The maximum effect can often be gained if your hand-eye coordination is good enough to allow you to take the ball late. This can encourage or trick the opponent into moving too early, providing the opportunity to send the ball another way.

Disguise with the arm can be used to 'show' one kind of shot, while producing another. For instance, you can show a full backswing, but stop the follow-through, turning a potentially full-blooded drive into a delicate drop shot. Qamar Zaman has been the master of this. A few players are strong and skilful enough to show no arm movement, no backswing. This suggests the ball will be pushed short, but instead it is flicked to a length. Nobody did this better than Hiddy Jahan.

Sleight of foot sounds almost like an absurdity, but it can be a subtle deception indeed. Many shots, particularly on the forehand side, can be played off either foot. By taking

7. Deception can be brought about by sleight of hand, wrist, arm and even foot or body. Qamar Zaman somehow manages all five at the same time

8. Opposite page: *The most frequent method of deception is late movement of the wrist. Jahangir Khan has his opponent rooted with this inventive backhand*

9. *Flicking the ball to a length, using the wrist and no backswing and concealing the intended direction – Hiddy Jahan using his famous shot against Ahmed Safwat*

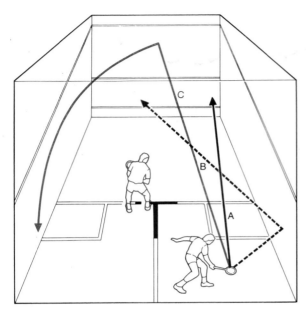

Diagram 1. Forehand back corner – three disguises with body masking racket (A : straight drive, B: boast, C: cross-court flick)

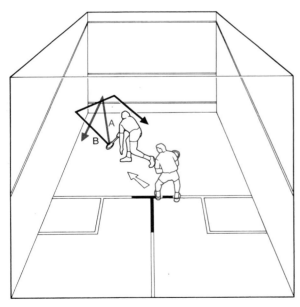

Diagram 2. Backhand front corner – two disguises with body masking racket (A: nudge down the wall, B: trickle boast round walls)

advantage of this, the same shot can be made to look different. Reading the direction of it can be made harder for the opponent. This can be an automatic deception once the technical requirements of playing off either foot have been mastered. A more deliberate deception is created by putting the front foot in one direction, and hitting the ball in another. Again, this is better done on the forehand.

Masking the ball with the body can be done equally well on the backhand and forehand. It is most likely to be achieved when striking the ball near to one of the corners with the opponent near the 'T' in the centre of the court. Sometimes he can be prevented from seeing the contact point at all. Thus he may find it hard to move until after the ball has been struck. From the backhand back corner a stroke may be a drive or a boast; from the forehand back corner it may be either of these or a cross-court flick as well (see diagram 1); and from the front corners a stroke may be a nudge down the wall towards the nick or a trickle round the walls that will end up on the other side of the striker's body (see diagram 2). Without seeing the wrist or hand of the striker, the opponent will be rooted, or guessing.

Sometimes deception can be achieved without placing this cloak over proceedings. It comes from what is sometimes called 'shot selection'. This can mean changes of pace as well as changes in the patterns used in similar situations. Shot selection is almost too facile a description of something which merges with the most profound tactical considerations. Despite this, it is worth remembering that a long-term, almost imperceptible form of deception is created by using an unexpected choice of shot. You will need a good memory for what strokes have been used before, and good intuition of when to change strokes.

There are always at least two possibilities for deception, even when you are penned into the back corners. The further you go up the court the more the possibilities increase. Once you get near to the short line there is little limit to the range of shots that can be produced.

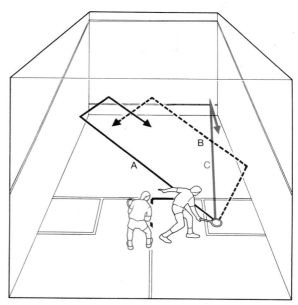

Diagram 3. Disguises from three-quarter length (A: reverse angle, B: boast, C: straight drive or straight drop)

10. *Jahangir's older brother Torsam Khan cleverly masks the direction of this backhand drop with his body. Ahmed Safwat tries to puzzle out what he is doing.*

From the most disadvantageous position – the back corner – the best deception is to show as if to hit down the wall and instead hit hard across court. Sometimes if the ball comes off the back wall a little way and it is a half to three quarter length, you can throw a reverse angle into the melting pot (see diagram 3). Players sometimes don't try this because of the risk of hitting the opponent.

If there is enough room, you can show a drive down the wall or across court, but instead hit a very low boast. You should quickly learn the positions from which this shot can turn into a three-wall boast, with a chance of ending up as a nick (see diagram 4). A three-wall boast will

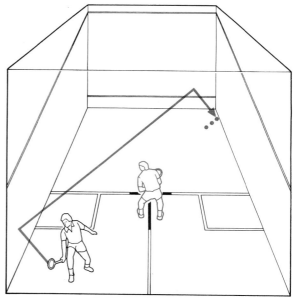

Diagram 4. Three-wall boast

really jerk your opponent forward because it can fall very short and die quickly. Even if your opponent reaches it, he or she may lift the ball up for you to get in and volley.

Another extremely valuable deception from the difficult back corner position can be achieved when the ball goes through quite strongly to the back wall. Provided it will come off the wall a short distance, allow it to drop almost for a second bounce. Ease the racket underneath and slice it with plenty of follow-through. This can create a beautiful straight drop shot down the wall. Even if the opponent reaches it he or she may not be able to do much provided the ball stays close to the wall. Should there be room on the backswing to show as if to make a powerful drive, so much the better.

Another variation, which is a Qamar Zaman speciality, is to let the ball pass the body deep in the forehand back corner, then send it cross-court just when it looks as though there is no room to do so. It is hit so late that the body masks the ball; it requires a flexible wrist plus great touch. The secret is to hit with plenty of slice; this keeps the ball on the strings longer, and makes a difficult shot easier. Zaman used to make it look so simple that even when his opponent was perfectly positioned on the 'T', the ball might go for a winner.

When you yourself are on the 'T', all sorts of things become possible. The lid of the box can be opened up on a whole range of tricks. There is one particularly valuable shot – a cross-court angled slice – that has come more and more into use in the top-level game. It ends up dying somewhere near the nick.

First, though, it is best to create the right conditions for this telling shot. Show the opponent a pattern, and then bluff. The first time the ball comes nicely into the middle of the court, try to kill it in the forehand front corner, using the nick. Even if you only slice it down hard, so that it strikes the sidewall first, it is still a good shot. Do this several times when the situation repeats itself. Then, when it comes to a crucial point, with your opponent under pressure,

show as if to play the same shot again – and let the snake out of the bag. At the last moment change the wrist slightly so that you play across court. It doesn't go deep and it doesn't go hard. But it goes low, and slithers away from your opponent, threatening to go to earth in the service box somewhere near the side wall.

This can be a particularly effective bluff (see diagram 5). It is tempting to employ it often. But use it with discretion and time it carefully for its most effective use. If you frequently use it, your opponent will learn to be on guard.

Set out to make your opponent forget this shot. This can be done by introducing another variation. Show as if to produce the same shot as usual but turn the wrist inside the ball instead of round the outside. It will become a fast boast.

This can also be done when you are right at the front of the court. Show as if to hit the ball hard as usual, and boast it instead, but a much gentler boast this time. Take the pace off the

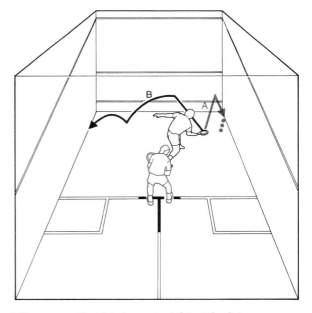

Diagram 5. Combining a straight nick, driven or dropped, with disguised cross-court slice, with *second* bounce dying in the nick (A : straight drive or drop, B: masked cross-court slice)

ball by slicing it, but the arm will follow through fast to help create disguise. The ball trickles round the side wall to the front wall, leaving the opponent wrongfooted. It should die in a position where you are roughly between the ball and the opponent. If he (or she) has gone the wrong way, he will be obliged by the rules to go round you (see diagram 6).

If you make the deceptions on the first and second stages, you can set up a whole chain of deceptions. Then you can start to dominate your opponent psychologically. Psychological guesswork – or intuition – plays an important part in those initial deceptions.

Another deception that can be used in the front court played an important part in the defeat of Jansher Khan in the World Open final of 1988 in Amsterdam. Jansher had won a month earlier in Monte Carlo from two games down and 3 – 3 in the third by dint of superior fitness. He may have had the capacity to do so again. But when the match reached a similar score he was beaten by two variations that helped turn the match.

They were reverse angles, both from short situations where a drop or an attempted kill had been the previous pattern (see diagram 7). It emphasized the value of keeping a trick in your pocket. They were played by getting down low, and using plenty of backswing and movement of the body to suggest a hard drive. Instead, the wrist and the racket were whipped across the body to pull the ball quickly on to the side wall. It died faster and shorter than any drop shot would have done, and Jansher was rooted, unable to read it. This is a risky deception, but there can be certain moments, such as these, when it is worth attempting.

The other, subtler variation of this reverse angle, is achieved by shaping to play a drop shot, and instead getting the ball narrowly to miss striking the front wall first. (Look at what happens, compared with the reverse angle, in diagram 8.) It appears from the way the stroke is formed that it will hit front wall first and drop near the nick. Instead it hits the side wall six inches or so from the front wall, and moves

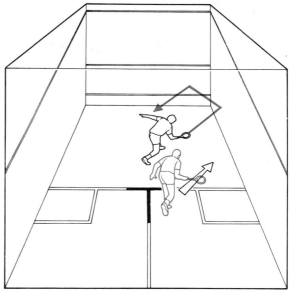

Diagram 6. Trickle boast sends opponent the wrong way, with striker positioned between ball and opponent after his wrong movement. He now has to go round the striker

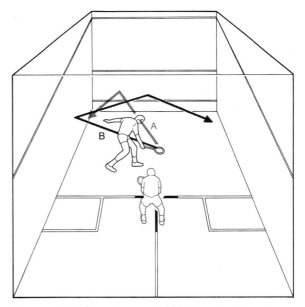

Diagram 7. Jahangir's crucial bluff against Jansher in the 1988 World final (A: previous pattern forehand drop, B: winning disguised reverse angle from front court)

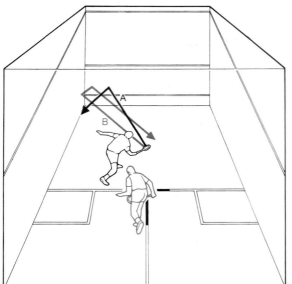

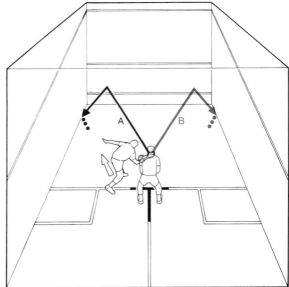

Diagram 8. Subtle variation of front court disguised reverse angle. The ball is played on to the side wall, inches from the join with the front wall (A: previous pattern, forehand drop, B: wrong-footing disguise, sending the ball in the other direction)

Diagram 9. Body not only masks direction of drop, but also moves in the direction of the bluff (A: previous direction and now the bluff, B: new direction of disguised drop)

back out to the middle of the court. It can wrongfoot your opponent just enough, perhaps causing him or her to move the wrong side of you, so having to go round you to get back. It is particularly effective on a glass court, where it is harder to see the ball until the last second.

Disguise of body and backswing can also be employed with the drop shot. By transferring the weight from back to front foot and moving the hips, and by bringing the racket down fast, the stroke can look like a certain drive. The secret is to keep the racket moving fast, rather than stopping it at the last moment, and turning the bottom edge underneath the ball in a heavy slice. This drags it down quite short after the spinning ball has struck the front wall.

An even better disguise of the body – body masking – can be used if the ball comes into the right position in the front court (see diagram 9).

This places the body completely between opponent and ball. By pressing and bending forward it looks as though the drop shot is going across court. But the opponent cannot see the impact or the follow-through, and the racket is taken inside and under the ball, making the stroke into a drop shot down the wall.

There is an easy routine that should enable you to practise all these front court disguises. The coach throws the ball up to be hit, calling out 'cross-court' or 'boast', or 'reverse angle' or 'drop'. The player does not know which he must hit until the command is given, which should increase his ability to play with a wide variation at the last possible second. The player hits down the wall if there is no command, and shows as if to hit down the wall on all the strokes until the command is given. However, it is almost impossible to recreate a match situation completely. This is because all shots have to be played against the opponent's position. An awareness of where he (or she) is, and where he is more likely to move, is essential. Lateral vision, hearing, and instinct, have to be finely tuned.

If the lower, 17-inch tin stays on the world circuit of the men's game, or even spreads to other levels, these deceptions will be more important still. The ability to use them is related to being on the balls of the feet, to being pre-pared to move early (usually forward), and to anticipation. These all help to heighten perceptions. It is also related to a slightly mysterious quality, sometimes called flair. This can be something to do with the player's personality as well as his or her capacity for skills.

But natural flair or no natural flair, the value of practice is often underestimated. Practice is the irrigation of the talents. With plenty of it, it is amazing what can be made to flower.

11. *The ability to use a variety of deceptions is related to being on the toes, prepared to move early*

3. Hitting Harder

12. Heather McKay, the hardest hitter.

Heather McKay was without any doubt the greatest woman player of all time. She dominated the game for two entire decades, and was still good enough at the age of 39 to win the inaugural women's World Championship. After that she retired to take up racketball, becoming the best player within a year. Such phenomenal success was based on the possession of a large number of qualities, not least a determinedly competitive temperament and strict attention to fitness — all the more remarkable in someone who started out as a heavy smoker! But probably what enabled her most of all to remain unbeaten between the acquisition of her first British Open in 1962 and her retirement in 1979 was the pace of her hitting. Particularly on the forehand she possessed the ability to drive through her opponents' defences, and that caused her to inflict even on her nearest rivals extraordinarily one-sided defeats. Altogether she won sixteen successive British Open titles, before deciding not to play in the event any more, giving encouragement to other younger players who represented the game's future

Hitting Harder

Hitting hard can be exciting, especially for men. The ball screeches as it hits the wall and whistles away at a satisfying speed. It can be effective too. Nobody who saw me play Jahan in the Pakistan Open final of 1982 would deny that. Rarely have so many points been won with so many clean winners.

However, you need to be careful. If you haven't the accuracy, the harder you hit the worse you'll be, as the more the ball will come out into the middle. Then if your opponent puts it away you'll look a bit of a macho moron.

Therefore make sure you hit hard to the right target and at the right time. This often means making the opening first; otherwise the ball travels like a bullet but doesn't go anywhere. In tennis you can put maximum power into it and it stays hit. In squash it simply stays in the squash court. The walls can destroy opponents or make it easy for them.

Two of the major advantages of hitting hard are, first to tire the opponent by the speed with which you are making him stretch; then to create an unexpected change of pace after which to ram a winner or near-winner through the hint of an opening. These two scenarios have become more and more important in the modern game.

This is partly due to the development of synthetic rackets. Materials such as graphite, kevlar and boron have enabled players to hit the ball harder and have helped change the way squash is played. By and large it has become a faster, lower game. There is a far greater range of rackets, enabling players to experiment and find what suits them best. The weapons are much more sophisticated. Almost everyone can fire rockets now.

Good Timing

The single most important factor is timing. This helps you not to be wasteful in your hitting. It is partly a mysterious thing as some players seem to possess good timing naturally, like a gift from God. Others have to develop it — but it is perfectly possible to do this.

What makes timing good or bad is often your reflexes. These must provide different responses in very different situations. For instance, if the ball is hit from 30 feet away towards the front wall and it is rebounding, there is no rush. If you are standing three yards from the front wall and the ball is hit the same way, the response must be dynamic. Some players actually seem to find it easier to react quickly.

If you have a good all-round technique, prepare early, and don't snatch, it is more likely that your reflexes will work to their maximum ability. Fitness also plays a part. The biggest hindrance is snatching, and it will happen more often if you are tired or anxious.

Power is only obtained by those who can perform a throwing action well. You cock the wrist and break it as you throw the racket forwards. The main question then is whether your wrist is controlled and strong enough to send the ball in the right direction. To do that the wrist has to be snapped and locked in the right position.

No good doing it if you are going to spray the ball around the court like bullets from a machine gun. There is a knack; work at developing it.

13. *Power through locking the wrist in the right position on the backhand drive. A moment of concentrated effort in one of the Khan clashes between Jahangir and Jansher*

Body Weight

Even if your reflexes and wrist-snap are not as good as they might be, you can develop a heavy shot by getting your weight into it. This means turning the body so that you are half facing the back wall on the forehand side, perhaps standing 45 degrees to the back wall. And on the backhand you should ideally turn even further, maybe even facing the back wall (see diagram 10). Some players stand sideways on the forehand, which is not good enough, unless they swivel their upper body and shoulder.

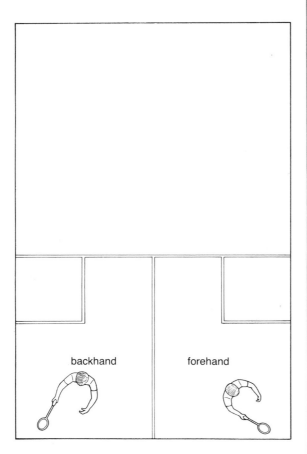

Diagram 10. Turn you back almost 45° to the front wall for a forehand drive and almost completely to the front wall for a backhand drive

14. *To develop a heavy shot, turn the back 45° to the front wall as Jahangir does here against Jansher. Notice the goldfish bowl feeling of playing inside an all-transparent court*

You can't do this properly unless your footwork is good. This is one of the reasons why a small player can sometimes hit the ball harder than a big one. If you arrive in time to become motionless for a fraction of a second before striking the ball, your timing may improve. If you are stetching most of the time you will be wasting power.

15. *Another view of a powerful Jahangir forehand, where extra weight of shot has been gained by turning the back at an angle to the front wall. This also helps mask the ball, making it hard for Phil Kenyon to see, despite his perfect positioning*

Opposite page: 16. *The backhand drive is often hit hardest when the back is completely turned on the front wall*

If you hit well, you usually transfer your weight well. This should become a natural process. You should not have to think about transferring weight from the back foot to the leading foot unless there is something wrong with your game. If you arrive too early and become statuesque, for instance, may become surprisingly impotent. Develop a flow and continuity between footwork and weight transference. Good balance will help you do that.

Opposite page: 17. *Transferring her weight well, Australia's Sarah Fitzgerald, with a forceful forehand. Notice the position of the right shoulder*

Below: 18. *Compare Jahangir's up-the-handle grip here with with Jansher's more conventional grip in photo 19. Jahangir's tends to create more control at the expense of power. (Fritz Borchert)*

Below right: 19. *Jansher's butt-of-the-hand on butt-of-the-handle grip. Contrast it with Jahangir's in photo 18. This is the grip usually recommended by coaches. It helps create a fuller arc on the swing and more power (Fritz Borchert)*

Grip

The grip can affect how hard you are able to hit. If you are going to give it a bit extra, your grip will need tightening. Some players have an open grip with the fingers spreading up the handle. It is alright to do this if you are playing a drop shot, but if you are going to let one rip with the fingers spread, you may feel you cannot hold the racket properly. To a certain extent the muscles will tighten up automatically and enable you to grip more as you perform the hitting action.

It is acceptable to have different grips and to experiment with them. Players won't have identical grips because their muscles are developed differently. Sometimes top players move the grip up and down the handle a little, perhaps because they feel stale and want to put something new into the game. But in theory the ball will be hit harder if the grip is as far down the racket as possible, i.e. with the butt of the hand on the butt of the handle. That way the length of arm and amount of leverage on the ball is increased.

Rhythm

Rhythm provides a creative link between grip, movement, and timing. It creates a harmonious relationship between all parts of the body, the racket and the ball, and it helps you strike the ball more freely. To achieve this it is necessary to relax. When you manage this your senses are likely to be heightened and the body is more flexible. Putting it another way: tension stops you from hitting the ball hard.

Tension can take on a mental or physical form. The warm-up can help remove both. Make sure that you perform a full quota of warming-up exercises before the knock-up. Then it is possible to hit hard right from the beginning of the match. It also helps take away nervousness and ensures you are on the ball immediately.

If you are warmed up, prepared, and in rhythm, the ball will heat up quickly. Hitting hard from the start will make the ball hotter and more responsive. If the ball is cold mistakes are more likely to be made. If it is warm, control is easier, and if it is very hot and bouncy, it may suit the fitter player.

Other Tips

It is essential for rhythm and timing that you do not swipe or snatch. This may seem like a beginner's error, but when fatigued and desperate it can happen. Stroke the ball with economy. Think about an image of the correct shot. And as you experience more pressure, physically or mentally, try to watch the ball more carefully. This will help avoid the slight mistimings that can put you on the receiving end in a rally.

If it begins to happen, there are several things you can do. Make sure your head is over the ball. For a few strokes, slow it down and stroke the ball more smoothly. Improve the timing before you increase the pace of your hitting again. By tossing the ball up a little more, and then weighing into it again, you can also create

a deceptive change of pace.

If you are hitting from the back you will need to strike the ball flat to gain the necessary pace and the right trajectory. Not many players can do this and get the ball to die on the second bounce, so they open the racket face and hit the ball higher on the front wall. If you do this, and then try a hard shot not too high on the front wall which bounces near the service box, you can sometimes get your opponent into trouble.

Judging the height of the trajectory, therefore, is vital. If you are halfway up the court, hit the ball about a foot above the tin. In the back corner, many players aim for a foot or two below the service line (see diagram 11). Even so, from this position it is sometimes worth trying a harder, lower shot. Indeed that may be necessary if the opponent on the 'T' is threatening to cut the ball off with a boast or straight drop.

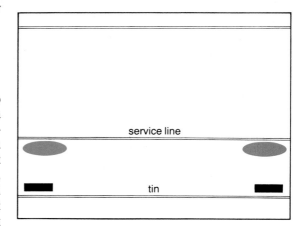

Diagram 11. Where to strike the ball on the front wall. The red areas are the targets from the back of the court on a straight drive; the black areas are the targets from half-court on a straight drive

20. Rhythm helps create a harmonious relationship between all parts of the body, the racket and the ball

Routines

Try the following a practice to develop the ability to hit harder. Adopt a standing position to facilitate the perfect transference of weight, then gradually begin moving. Stand close to the side wall in the forehand front corner and move back, returning the ball to yourself. Build up power gradually and accurately, making sure the ball goes down the wall. You need a steady wrist to do this.

Another good routine is to stand on the 'T' facing the back wall and hit forehands on to the forehand wall. As the ball comes back to you, hit backhands on to the backhand wall. Repeat this, building up the power. Without a combination of accuracy and power the ball will not return to you. The more accurate you become the more you will be able to stand still and develop strength of shot.

If you do this conscientiously it will add invaluable penetration to your game. Listen to the sound of the ball. It should give you an idea of whether you are hitting the ball as hard on the forehand as on the backhand. If not, then you may have a weakness which can be worked upon.

Many players lack the strength or timing to dig the ball out of the back backhand corner. The best practice for this is to stand behind the service box and hit the ball down the wall by yourself. Hit really hard to develop strength, using a full follow-through. Once you have mastered this, hit down the wall so that the ball reaches the back wall. Then hit the side of the ball to make a boast. The ball will come low and you will have to hit hard. You can also do this routine with a partner, who plays down the wall while you boast.

Many players have their positioning wrong and get too close to the ball. To hit the ball with maximum power there must be enough room for the swing. When boasting you can move sideways and almost be facing the back wall. If there isn't room to swing you may have to jab up the back of the ball, throwing it straight on to the front wall. But usually there is more room than you think in which to make the shot.

Women

Hitting harder can be a problem for women. Sometimes it is due to a lack of wrist-snap, creating a kind of pushing action. Wrist-snap can be difficult to achieve if it doesn't come naturally. The best way is to develop the ability to throw. Throw a ball. Drop all the weight on to the foot on the side that is holding the ball, and hurl the ball with the elbow first bending and then jerking straight. The desired action with the squash racket, although it is under-arm, is similar to this.

Another teaching aid is to think about punching and pressing the ball on impact. Remember that there is more follow-through on the forehand. Where the follow-through on the backhand finishes, the follow-through on the forehand starts.

Having an extra hard shot in your repertoire can win you points or create openings. You will find it especially effective if you hit a cross-court drive with change of pace. This may prevent your opponent from playing strokes, and can force mistakes. It may work best off a short ball. Heather McKay, the world's best player for two decades, was particularly good at this.

21. *Jahangir shows how to develop power with the help of a full but not excessive follow-through*

22. *Think about punching or pressing on impact.*
This photo excellently captures Jahangir's
moment of contact with the ball

4. Movement

23. Aman Khan, the fleet-footed.

Aman Khan who was good enough at tennis to play Davis Cup for Pakistan, decided along with his brother Rahmat to turn to top-class squash in the early 1970s. He reached the world's top twenty with a style of play characterized by superbly light-footed court coverage. No one was better balanced, or covered the court with a more effective long stride. But making a living as a professional player at that time was almost impossible and after mixing competition with coaching for a while, Aman set out to emulate his famous father Nasrullah Khan and become a full-time coach. He rapidly made a name for himself at the Albany Club in Birmingham, where his patience, skill, and clever psychology made him as valuable to child beginners as to established players like David Lloyd, Fiona Geaves and Lisa Opie. Aman also did clinics with Jonah Barrington and with Rahmat in different parts of Europe and the Middle East before moving to the Bath and Rackets Club in London. He remains as slim and light-footed as ever

Movement

Move badly and you probably play badly too. Continue to move badly and you may do yourself lasting physical harm. But move well and all things are possible. Movement is the prerequisite for everything; indeed of all the racket sports, squash more than any other has movement at its core.

However, understanding movement is not easy. It requires a comprehension of footwork, balance, weight transference, and even rhythm. There are different types of footwork, depending on the situation. And sometimes

Below left: 24. *Jahangir going for a front court forehand on the correct (i.e. left) foot. This should help create maximum balance and control. Compare with photo 25 where he uses the 'wrong' foot*

Below: 25. *Jahangir's 'wrong' (i.e. right) foot is used to reach this ball in the front forehand corner. Although this may be harder to do, it can cause more uncertainty for the opponent. From this position it is hard to tell whether he is hitting the ball short or long, to the forehand or backhand*

interesting choices have to be made between right and 'wrong' footwork.

Underlying all this is fitness. None of the lunges, chassis movements, small steps, or gobbling strides can be done for any length of time without basic strength or stamina. Indeed to attempt such things without having prepared properly is to increase the risk of injury. By the time you come to think about improving your movement on court you should have done some background long distance work to increase your strength; then perhaps some sprints or interval 400 metres to improve your speed, and speed-with-stamina.

Footwork is important for the process of developing strokes. You may not be able to hit the ball properly if you are off balance. The really gifted players, however, may not have a problem here as their ability enables them to hit the ball whilst standing on one leg if necessary, and this can even be an advantage because of the deception it creates. It is possible to play several shots off the 'wrong' foot and it is sometimes worthwhile good players trying routines to develop this.

As a general rule it is best to take medium strides rather than long ones, as this avoids stretching the muscles which can be very fatiguing. If you are in control of the rally, or sparring equally with your opponent, you can often use small, quick steps to go to the back corners

Below: 26. *Jahangir is going for a front court backhand with the 'wrong' (i.e. left) foot. It may look as though he is going to hit across court with this footwork: a flick down the wall may wrongfoot the opponent. Compare with photo 27*

Below right: 27. *Jahangir's footwork forward with the right (correct) leg looks more comfortable on the backhand. He may find it easier to maintain accuracy like this*

and return to the 'T' without running at all. This is stepping in balance, and the effort is minimal. Mohibullah Khan used to walk and for that he took slightly longer steps. But quick walking is best, and certainly far better than running.

Much used to be written about the gobbling stride – one long stride followed by another to cover the ground in the minimum number of strides. Since such advice was given there have been great advances in deception in the top level of the game, and that method of movement may not be quite so appropriate. The best advice is therefore to move in the most balanced way in order to apply the best disguise to your shot. If you rush to one corner and rush back, you sometimes don't even know what step you are taking.

However, sometimes long strides may be necessary, particularly if you are forced to retrieve. In such cases it can be remarkable just how far you can go in two strides. From the 'T' position you can cover the majority of the court, and it will need a good shot to one of the four corners to require you to take a third or fourth stride.

Hopefully this will not happen too often, as it can be tiring. More frequently you may need to produce one last long stride, a lunge, usually to reach a drop shot at the front. The lunge will also help you get maximum leverage with your arm and thus more power.

Diagram 12. The chassis movement towards the forehand back corner. First the left foot is drawn up to the right foot, and then the right foot is drawn away again. The body moves sideways

Chassis

A chassis (see diagram 12) is particularly valuable when moving to the back or middle of the court on the forehand side. It enables you to keep your eye on the ball and, out of the corner of your eye, on the opponent at the same time.

28. Sometimes long strides are necessary to retrieve. Sometimes expedience is necessary too – Jahangir has moved forward with the 'wrong' foot. Despite this he maintains good balance

It is quite a comfortable way of moving, although it will mean you hit the forehand off the 'wrong' foot. This will enable you to hit cross-court more easily, and later with more disguise, as well as down the wall. On the backhand it is very difficult to chassis across and prepare properly for the stroke, as there is no room for a backswing. A backhand almost always requires you to play off the correct foot, half turning your back to the front wall.

However, you should be in a position to hit a backhand boast after a chassis. In mid-court,

you will be able to do an attacking boast, or, if you have good wrist work, to dig the ball out late in the back court. The beauty of the chassis is that it is easy to return quickly to the 'T', using the same movements in reverse.

However, you may lose power if you use the chassis and hit off the 'wrong' foot. With the correct footwork you will be able to wind up further, to lean back and forwards as you hit and to keep the ball low. The trouble is that a boast off the correct foot, with the body turned right round, may telegraph your intentions. If your opponent then moves early to anticipate it you can be in trouble – unless you boast the ball into the nick. By boasting off the 'wrong' foot you keep the opponent back on the 'T' until your shot is played, particularly on the forehand.

Preparation

One of the most important functions of good footwork is to prepare you properly; but to do that you need to move early. This implies a good stance and a good ready position. It is a little like the runner in a 100-metre race: if you are not settled properly on the starting blocks you may lose the race.

The ready position should not be static. As your opponent hits the ball you give a little hop. This is crucial. It gets you started and bounces your body so that further motion comes more fluently and easily. Try it and see. Moving away from a standing start feels, by comparison, as though your feet are tied down.

Many leading players have the racket dangling quite low when waiting on the 'T', although this is not really advisable. By all means adopt a stance that combines comfort with the maximum ability to make a quick getaway. But if the head of the racket is too low, it

29. *In two long strides from the 'T' you can cover wide areas of the court. Qamar Zaman here shows how far you can reach with one long early stride. Phil Kenyon is the alert opponent*

30. *Qamar Zaman has done a chassis and is about to play a shot off the 'wrong' foot which has kept Phil Kenyon rooted. It is impossible to tell whether Qamar will drive, drop, boast or flick the ball across the court*

Opposite page: 31. *Lucy Soutter's state of readiness could hardly be bettered as Liz Irving plays a backhand. As well as bouncing slightly on the balls of her feet Soutter has the racket head up in the recommended position*

may make it harder for you to address the ball properly, especially under pressure. When you are getting tired it can pay dividends to keep the racket up, to enable a smooth and early preparation, and avoid snatching at the ball.

That first stride is very important. Invest effort in making it early and you should get returns in saved energy and will avoid being jerked around the court. Watch players who have good footwork and see how they anticipate where and when to go. Jansher Khan and Chris Robertson do this and so did Geoff Hunt.

Be critical, too. For instance, Hunt's footwork was so nimble that he could nearly always get to the ball in time to hit a forehand in the correct position with the left foot forward. This made him easier to read: either he was playing down the wall or hitting a boast. On the other hand players like Hiddy Jahan, Mohibullah Khan and Qamar Zaman have often gone in on the 'wrong' foot, with the opponent on the 'T', however well prepared he is, left wondering what was going to happen.

Aman Khan also has particularly good footwork. He is lightly built, which can be helpful. The trimmer you become and the lighter on your feet, the more balanced your movement is likely to be. If you are heavy and having to put more effort into your recovery, then the greater your chance of sustaining injury. So weight reduction and good footwork can be an insurance policy.

Use of the 'T'

Good footwork is also useful for the service, because you need to make the movement from the service box to a place somewhere near the central 'T' junction as smoothly and as easily as possible. Where that place will be will depend upon the circumstances of the situation and who you are playing.

For instance, if your serve has come off the side wall to somewhere near the middle at the back, then there is no way you can occupy the 'T' at all. You will be in the way. It is important

therefore to get a service that stays reasonably close to the corners, combining it with a movement that takes you naturally sideways and into the middle in two steps.

If your opponent has a very good short game then you may want to move forward on to the 'T' itself. But generally, when the length game to the back is being played, you will take up a position further back, perhaps two to three feet behind the 'T'. Occasionally you even see players further back, but in that situation they would need to be very sharp and fast in moving forward.

Shadow Training

To be able to do all these things, shadow court training is important and greatly improves footwork. The coach calls out a number which corresponds to an area of the court, and the player has to move to it and back again quickly. This is repeated using all the areas on the court as an unpredictable sequence.

Running and skipping are also vital. They strengthen the legs and thereby automatically improve balance and recovery. Exercises involving standing on one leg, or hopping, are also good. Try walking forwards and backwards, then do it with the maximum amount of stretch, with arms outwards as if walking on a tightrope. The object is to build up balance, not speed.

Some players have a natural ability to move with economy; others don't. Two players can cover the same distance by using varying amounts of energy. If it is not natural for you to move economically, think about it and try some of the ideas suggested here. Develop a style of movement that is comfortable and adaptable. It needs to change according to the situation on court. Above all you should be trying to capture that elusive thing – a knack.

32. *Anticipate and you will move early. Move early and you will save energy – like Chris Robertson*

5. Pressure

33. Geoff Hunt, the pressure soaker.

*Few men soaked up pressure better than Geoff Hunt, who
established a record of eight British Open titles when he narrowly
beat Jahangir in the famous British Open final of 1981. Physically
Hunt could endure as long as any player in the history of squash,
while mentally he was able to get himself into prime condition for
matches he really wanted to win. In that '81 final, for instance, he
had looked too ill to go on and afterwards was passing blood. But
he came back from 1-6 down in the fourth game to win in nearly
two and a quarter hours. Throughout 1979 he was repeatedly
beaten by the brilliant Qamar Zaman and was deposed as top seed
in his attempt to win the title for the sixth time. But he duly
triumphed again, beating Zaman 3-1 in the final, and once more
raising his game to new levels on the big occasion with an
adherence to the basic virtues of good line and length. (Incidentally
Jahangir got his own back by beating Hunt in the 1981 World Final,
and went on to overtake the great Australian's record of eight
British Open titles in 1990)*

Pressure

Battles are lost and won away from the court as well as inside it. Mountains are climbed inside the mind as well as by the body. Many are the squash players who, when practising, have combined the qualities of a technician with those of an artist. But when they compete, they crumble. Competition creates pressure; and pressure teaches us all something about ourselves.

Top-level sport creates some of the most intense pressure of all. A great emotional investment has been made in order to achieve a high level of skill. Much of it has to be realized at a specific time, often with many people watching and sometimes without a second chance. A sportsman or woman has to succeed, which makes him or her vulnerable. There is great pressure, both mental and physical: pressure created by the opponent and pressure created by the self. It is also brought about by the occasion and the state of the match. Pressure is usually necessary to bring out the best in a really top-class player, but it can boil up and become too hot to handle, sometimes without the player being aware of what is happening. There is a fine line between the pressure that makes you do better and that which destroys you.

Do you feel nervous before matches? If so, you should also feel reassured. You are keyed up – you need to be to perform well. It is the extent of the nervousness and how well you control it which matters most. Nervousness can be controlled by acquiring as much match practice as possible. Exposure to tension-making situations, in matches that do not matter so much, should reduce your sensitivity and increase your ability to handle the pressures.

Learn the best way to handle them. Do you like to go away by yourself and be quiet before matches? Or do you like to have someone talk it over with you? Whichever is better for you, make sure you do it. Carefully thinking out a match plan, preparing yourself for what to expect, and working out how to avoid mistakes made last time, can be a great help. Professionals usually like to avoid situations where chance remarks from onlookers and untimely offers of advice and encouragement can create unintended pressure.

Much pressure is self-created. This is a vast area about which a whole book could be written. The development of a self-knowledge, that difficult art, has to be practised. Of course, it can take a lifetime, but there is some learning that can be acquired quite quickly.

Develop realistic goals. Don't imagine you are a Geoff Hunt or a Jansher Khan. Making false comparisons or relying on dreams can bring about disappointments, which are damaging. Even if you are talented, goals which are appropriate for these great players may not be for you. Some players even create false impressions with stylish dress and equipment bearing famous names.

So be yourself. Visualize yourself as you will be after your next step of improvement. Aim for that. Be honest: draw up your practice plan or training plan and stick to it. Don't pretend to

34. *Pressure, both physical and mental, afflicts the top-class player – even if he is as good as Gawain Briars*

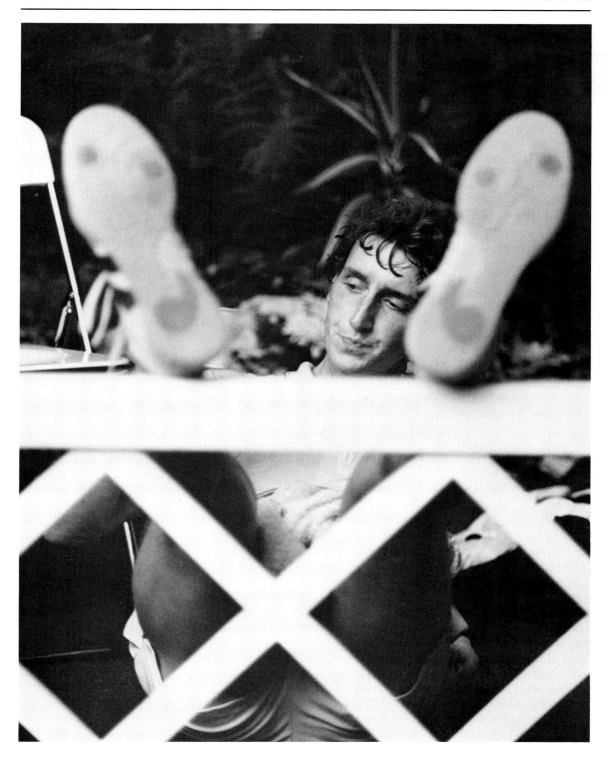

yourself or your coach that you have done things that you have not. You so obviously cheat yourself by doing this, although it is surprising how many players do.

Avoid negative thinking. This can be practised too: don't anticipate failure and never talk as though you expect it. Do things to the best of your ability even if it looks as though you may fall short of your goal. Concentrate less on the goal, and more on how you are getting there. By calm, constructive, positive attitudes you condition the unconscious mind and make it healthier. And it is the unconscious mind that has a hugely powerful influence over performance.

35. *Talking it over with a coach or trainer or helper can relieve pressure. This is Jahangir and Rahmat back in 1984*

Don't make excuses or alibis about losing before a match. This unwittingly creates more pressure, not less. If you determine to give of your best, but still lose, you have nothing with which to reproach yourself. Nor is one defeat necessarily important in the whole scheme of things. Many players make excuses after a defeat, as well as before, but this prevents the learning process. The best thing to do is to come out and say: the opponent was better than I was *today*. Don't accept he or she will be always better.

Negative attitudes can result from personal problems: injuries, finances, poor organization, or relationships. A sensible coach can often help with these. Wives/husbands or girl/boyfriends can create special pressure. To have an understanding spouse is marvellous, but even when you are in that fortunate situation there can still be small distractions – for instance whether he or she is properly accommodated in the auditorium. It is easy to start thinking about your spouse or partner in the back of your mind. Therefore, by and large, it may be advisable to keep these kinds of relationship separate from competitive squash.

True, both Gamal Awad and Phil Kenyon had wives who helped or even coached them. But if something goes wrong, it can cause tremendous frustration – and possibly enmity – which makes for the worst sort of pressure on court. Both JKs (myself and Jansher) have experienced the pressure of a partner of the opposite sex and the resulting problems, either real or imagined. It is fair to say that with both of us it has affected our squash. That should be a warning to other players.

The Jahangir story has seen both victory and defeat. For the first five and a half years there were all those wins, some hard, but many pretty easy really. And then, quicker than any of us could have expected, there were sudden defeats. There were eight in a row against Jansher. Remember those? A lot of players might have folded after that, particularly after being unbeaten for such a long time. But by creating the feeling that it was possible to come back, whatever the adversity, it is amazing what was achieved.

As common as psychological pressure is physical pressure, and it is sometimes hard to separate them. Each can act as a barometer of the other: tire and you worry, fret and you flag. But this interaction can be made to work in your favour. There are many stories of great players whose minds have made their bodies perform miracles.

The pressure of oxygen debt can make the legs wobble. But remember the Hunt/Barrington battles and the Hunt/Jahangir tussles, and think of my rivalry with Jansher. Sometimes what was achieved seemed to transcend the possible. Transcend is a good word; the mind has the power to do exactly that. We will return to this at the end of this chapter.

The door to the mind's wealth, however, can really only be opened with proper training. Training the body implicitly trains the mind. It also enables the body to keep going long enough to explore the limits of the mind under pressure. It develops the relationship between the two and strengthens it.

Training is, of course, a pressure in itself. You have to put yourself through long-distance running as a basic strength builder. This can hurt. It can also bore the mind. No coach or trainer can help; you can only conquer these things on your own. You will come to pain and boredom barriers when the mind must say: 'No! I shouldn't even slow down let alone stop.' Trying to keep your speed going provides the competition.

In a match, competition with the opponent will require you to keep your speed going and to maintain the quality of your game at the same time. There are tactics that can help you do this. First make sure you are properly warmed up before you start – warming-up may continue after the match begins. It can take a while to get used to the speed of the court, the bounce of the ball and the nature of the rallies. So it may be best to play conservatively to begin with, perhaps hitting the ball safely, a little higher on the front wall, until your control or length and line has developed.

This is a useful tip at any crisis point. If the match is running away from you or if it is necessary to cut down your error ratio, playing a few tight balls down the wall can steady things up both tactically and psychologically. Combined with economical court coverage it can give body and mind time to recover. Two early longish strides from the 'T' will enable you to reach a remarkably large area of the

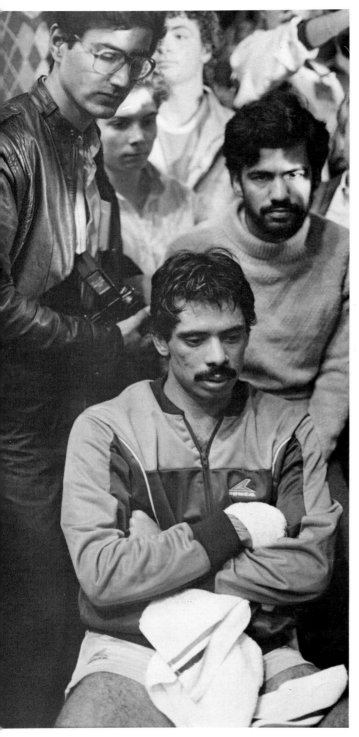

court in any direction. Neat movement and tight ball control can exert a containing and calming influence. Although this may appear self-evident to the observer, it is easy for the player to forget in the heat of the moment. Another way to focus your mind under pressure is to think of what you have produced in practice and in training, and to produce it again. The score, the situation, the atmosphere can distort your vision.

Sometimes players don't play well, and there does not appear to be an obvious reason why. That may be due to organizational worries. There are many of these, but one of the most common of them relates to money. Many good squash players have struggled financially, and some have given up.

Indeed, for the tournament player the first pressure is how to get sponsorship. By this we mean not so much the big equipment sponsors and endorsements for clothing and rackets, but the smaller sponsors that can enable players to start. They could come from a local garage or a small local company. It needs enterprise to dig them out, but without them it is difficult to give the game the time needed to reach the top.

Many players who cannot give their full time to squash have to coach, as Rahmat and Aman did, but if they do more than four hours of this a day it becomes too much. A player needs to spend between four and six hours a day on squash to have a chance of making the grade. As it is easy to become stale, having enough sponsorship to allow for a few hours' play each day without worrying about money can make all the difference. Then the player will get sufficient rest.

Lack of money and sponsorship can create false or short-term goals. Players may take part in tournaments that are of no great help to

36. *Jahangir has seen both victory and defeat. This picture was taken after the most famous defeat of all – the one that ended the longest ever unbeaten run of five years seven months and one day. It came against Ross Norman in 1986 in Toulouse*

them, just to get a little prize money. They may play in too many tournaments, getting tired and risking injury. Some may even play with injuries. Better to spend that time, if you are a good player, looking for a sponsor. Very often a little known company will not be aware of the advantages – so take time to write and explain. Small sponsors and up-and-coming players can often grow together and gain mutually.

Pace yourself. Plan carefully. Draw up a sensible schedule. Often it is better for players to have the burden of such decisions taken away from them. Even if they cannot afford to pay someone to do this, it is usually possible to find a friend or adviser with whom they can have a sensible and honest dialogue.

There are too many players who have to do everything for themselves – book tickets, fix hotels, decide where to go and how much to play. After a while the responsibilities can weigh them down. Ideally a coach-cum-mentor lightens these burdens, and can also be around to answer questions, particularly that question 'Why?' when things go wrong. A player usually needs somebody to understand, to help evaluate, and if necessary to take some of the feeling of blame.

However great the problems, a healthy mind can solve many of them. Making the most of the human mind, which appears to have almost limitless powers, is a great art. Some poeple spend a lifetime developing that art. They do so in a great variety of ways by using relaxation techniques, meditation, hypnotherapy, psychology, and yoga. All have their value. We believe that such methods are often related to prayer, and we would suggest you might consider this as well. Whatever method you use, it is wise to spend a little time in silence and contemplation. Allow the silt to sink to the bottom of the river. Clear the waters. Improve your vision. It is amazing what you can see.

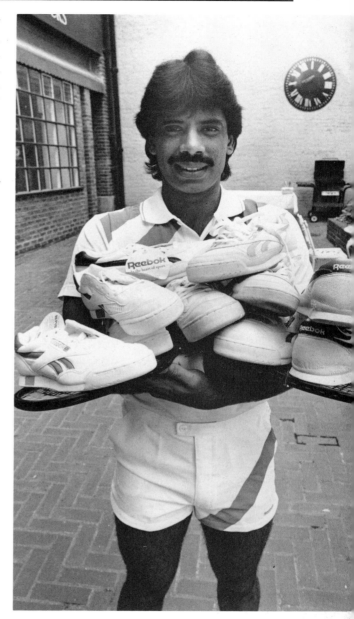

37. *Finding a sponsor certainly helps relieve pressure!*

SECTION II – Brushing Up Basics
6. The Drive

38. Jansher Khan, one of the game's best drivers.

Jansher Khan has helped create one of the most fascinating rivalries (with Jahangir) the game of squash has ever seen. He burst to the top in the second half of 1987 with a remarkably simple game based on tremendous mobility and accurate backhand and forehand drives, directed to a good line and length. That enabled him to beat Jahangir nine times out of ten and to become World Champion at the age of 18, before Jahangir caught up with him again and won the world title back in 1988. Part of his secret was an immaculate early preparation and a well-grooved swing, much in the manner of his elder brother Mohibullah Khan, once world number two. This economical method enabled Jansher to keep going even under great duress, as for example in the amazing final of the 1988 Swiss Masters. Then he came back from being match point down in the third game against Jahangir and saved another match point in the fifth game to win in two hours and ten minutes

The Drive

Sometimes you can get carried away. The more advanced you become the more you may lose sight of the basics. A return to them may pay dividends – the high-powered engine can do with a bit of servicing from time to time. More often, there will still be technical defects. It is remarkable how many players play to quite a high level with faults that need correcting.

These can perhaps be divided into three categories – the drive, the volley, and the short game. The foundation of the game, at any standard, is the drive. Let's do some servicing on that stroke first.

Check the backhand down the wall. In top-class squash this stroke is played more than any other. Even amongst many players who have been in the game for a long time, it can create problems: lack of strength compared with the forehand, for example, or even lack of control. Just controlling the ball up and down the backhand wall can be difficult for the less talented.

It is vital to practise it. Down the wall, down the wall – it can easily be done by yourself. If you are finding accuracy a problem, cut down the pace and ensure that you are hitting with a little slice. This will keep the ball on the racket face a bit longer and give more feel. You should be able to get the ball to travel parallel to the wall only a few inches from it. Make it bounce near the back of the service box to stop the volleyer.

The best practice for extra pace of shot is to stand near the back and hit to yourself, making sure that you use a full follow-through. Press into the ball as you make contact. Transfer weight forward into it. Prepare high and early.

Check back on all the working parts of the stroke.

Some players, even at a good standard, can have problems digging the ball out of the back corners, particularly on the backhand. Whether it is hooked out, driven out with a limited backswing, or boasted out, the stroke needs timing as well as strength.

Practise this in combination with good length drives on both backhand and forehand. Hit as hard as you can straight down the wall from behind the service box. Let the second bounce go on to the back wall, and take the ball as it comes off that wall. When you have done that twice, hit the third one hard into the side wall – a boast. You will build up your ability to hit the back of the ball and the side of the ball without making mistakes.

Notice your positioning. Are you getting too square on? (This would be fatal on the backhand, but can cost you weight of shot on the forehand as well.) If so, turn your back to the front wall more. It is very easy to get too close to the ball when it is in the corners, but you need to make enough room for a swing. Without telegraphing what you are going to do, it may be better to move sideways a little more if a boast is the shot you are about to play, because if you are almost facing the back you will have no angle through which to hit the ball.

Half turn your back to the front wall when playing a drive, particularly on the backhand; when you play the boast into the side wall on

39. *Prepare high and early like Jahangir does here, even with Jansher breathing down his neck*

the backhand you should turn your back almost completely. However, if the ball is too low in the corner then it is important to get down and retrieve the ball with a flick of the wrist. You need no backswing or follow-through to speak of, and you should come right under the ball with your racket. It can be done when there is almost no room at all.

Those are the three things, therefore, which can be practised using one basic exercise — flicking with the wrist, following through hard down the wall, and a proper follow-through on a side wall boast.

Until you get complete control on the boast, hit under the ball. This will send it higher and

40. *Half or completely turn your back for a backhand drive, like Lucy Soutter's neat preparation*

Opposite page: 41. *Follow through hard but economically, like Susan Devoy's strong backhand drive does here against Martine le Moignan*

ensure it does not end in the tin. Once you have more confidence with the shot, you can hit the ball flat and hard so that it does not lose height and retains its power. If you hit it low it will obviously stay low and may go from the front wall into the nick. This is the three-wall boast.

If you find the exercise described too demanding to do consistently, start by throw-

ing the ball into a back corner with the non-racket hand. From that you can try the flick, the straight drive or the boast. Or perhaps a partner can help. One very good routine is for one person to hit down the wall and the other to hit cross-court, and then to switch without stopping.

Try another routine. This is good for developing strength on a weaker wing. Stand in the middle of the court, behind the short line, parallel to the back of the service box, and in the area between the service boxes, but behind the 'T'. Then hit the ball with the forehand on to the backhand wall (the side wall) as hard as you can. The ball will hit the side wall and go over to the other wall, forehand side, and hit it just above the nick. Then hit a backhand on to that wall.

Forehand on to backhand wall, backhand on to forehand wall – keep the rhythm going. Judge for yourself by the impact noise how well you are hitting the ball. It should be roughly the same for both forehand and backhand. You can diagnose your own weakness.

Some people find that it is easier to wind up, get the shoulders round, and lay into the ball really hard on the forehand. On the backhand, they sometimes find that the upper body inhibits the backswing and transference of weight forward. The throwing action is also slightly unnatural on the backhand. With the whole hand behind the racket on the forehand the throwing action seems normal; on the backhand little is behind it, which may seem odd. Hence the need for more effort on that side.

Remind yourself that it is the same arm you are using for both backhand and forehand and when the ball comes, really smack into it. With the sort of practice routines we have mentioned there is not a lot of time for preparation, let alone for thinking about the weaker wing.

Try one other routine. It will help you drive more crisply. Stand in front of the 'T' in the front court. Turn slightly towards the wing where you are going to make the shot and hit the ball as hard as you can on to the front wall, about one foot away from the side wall. It is

directed as though you were trying to play a drop shot into the nick, except that you hit it about two feet above the tin. It then hits the side wall hard a short distance from the front wall and comes out towards the centre of the court, close to where you will be. Then you hit it again. It is an exercise in learning to prepare yourself quickly.

It is also important to do routines for the clinger. If you cannot make the ball cling to the wall, you are vulnerable to an opponent with attacking flair. Many players hit the ball flat, not realizing that the ball will not cling to the wall so well. If it's very tight on the side wall you have to hit it back flat. But if it's away from the wall you should open the racket slightly towards the side wall, giving it slight sidespin and underspin. The ball will go straight until it hits the front wall, then it will keep turning towards the side wall. By the time it has reached the back court the ball will be holding on to the wall, and the spin will make it cling there. The clinger is important, but people don't use it enough especially on the forehand. On the backhand it comes more naturally. You can put your opponent under considerable pressure by using it in the middle of a long rally. Although players are sometimes less accurate on the forehand side, there is actually more potential with the forehand clinger as the ball can be sliced more. With exactly the same action the ball can be played very gently and softly on to the side wall, creating a beautiful faded boast.

Different players use different grips on their basic drives. There are even a few who change grips, but I don't recommend it. Stick to one grip, close to the continental grip (as described in *Winning Squash*). You can alter the grip by twisting and turning the wrist to help direct the ball and obtain slice. If your wrist is cocked, it is easy to play under the ball on a drop shot.

42. *Some people find it easier to wind up and get the shoulders round on the forehand. Here Jahangir moves in but still stops quickly enough to allow sufficient distance between himself and the ball*

7. The Volley

43. Rahmat Khan, a good volleyer.

Some people forget that the man who coached Jahangir was once a good player himself. During the 1970s Rahmat reached the fringes of the world's top ten before deciding to concentrate on becoming the mentor of the greatest player of all time. This happened after Jahangir's elder brother Torsam (Rahmat's cousin and Amanat's father) died of a heart attack at the age of 28. Jahangir was already an outstanding prospect, but with Rahmat's support and advice he became World Champion in the incredibly short time of two years, by the age of 17. Rahmat's volleying skills had been a notable feature of his repertoire and he was able to act as a valuable sparring partner as well as coach. He had originally been a high standard tennis player and hence had learnt to take the ball early and look for opportunities to increase the pressure on his opponent. At his best he was able to trouble any leading player in the world; as a coach he was able to play a part in the downfall of every leading player in the world

The Volley

The volley is very important at a high level. In order to beat Jansher Khan, for instance, it is usually necessary to use it to move him around. But it is essential to do so at the right time – if you don't, you risk burning up unnecessary energy and running out of fuel before the end of the match. It is often very demanding to volley the ball early in a long match.

Good judgement is needed, and people have different ideas about this. Some players are prepared to invest the energy needed for a couple of volleys in order to bluff the opponent. When he or she hits the ball down the wall they cut it off, and either play it across court or hit it back to the opponent. There is no obvious gain. Then suddenly they will move early to the ball again and play it to the front, hoping that the opponent stays back. This can be a positive tactic, but sometimes it is done to play to the gallery, which is very foolish.

Otherwise, the right time to volley is when the opponent is already at the back. Play it to the front, either directly into the nick off the front wall or with a volley boast. You will be moving the opponent as much as possible, cutting down his recovery time and stretching his body. A volley can be done equally well on the backhand and forehand and is best taken from near the middle of the court. Sometimes it may be used again when the opponent has gone to the front, this time volley-driving him to the back. By then you are not only moving him around, you may be endeavouring to win the point outright.

Look for opportunities as well as trying to create them. It can be useful to volley if the opponent makes a cross-court drive when you are near the 'T'. In this situation it might be worth expending a little extra energy to reach the ball.

It is vital to practise the volley by yourself. The volley game can only be played well if the legs are strong, and a proper volley can only be made if the arms are strong. When a player hits the tin a lot with the volley, it's probably not because he (or she) has the wrong idea of how to play the shot: it's more likely to be because of insufficient strength in the arms.

Build up strength. Basic hitting of the ball, especially on the return of serve, is a good way of doing it. Many players don't have enough strength on the high backhand volley, with which returns of serve are often made. It may not be physical strength which is lacking. If you are forced by the position of a high ball to stand on one leg, your centre of gravity changes and strength is reduced. Develop strength of shot as well as muscular strength.

There is another routine which is good for developing the arms, as well as improving your eye for the volley. Stand in the middle of the front court, volleying across the body. The forehand volley is hit towards the backhand front corner, and the backhand volley towards the forehand front corner. Play these alternately, aiming the ball towards the joins of the front and the side walls. This will bring the ball back

44. *If you can cut off a cross-court you may be able to pressurize your opponent. So expending a little extra energy may be worthwhile, as Jahangir shows with this volley against Jansher*

45. *You can develop strength of shot with excellent footwork, balance and weight transference, as Jahangir does here, as well as through sheer muscular strength*

towards you in the middle, and enable you to continue rallying with yourself. You will need to prepare quickly, and quite soon it can become hard work. The volley should be struck in different ways. If you are hitting it low the impact needs to be flatter. If you are sending the volley high, say one foot below the out line, then you have to cut under the ball. This tends to bring it down, and helps prevent it going out at the side. If you are hitting a high volley downwards you may also want to slice the ball.

A good player should be able to play volleys into the nick. This can be the only sure way to end a rally against a high-class opponent who is fit and fast enough to reach everything. With practice this spectacular shot can be achieved a high percentage of the time. If it doesn't hit the nick, make sure it hits the side wall before it hits the floor, and it will stay lower and shorter.

Cross-court volley nicks can be risky if they are not played perfectly. On the cross-court backhand they can set up the opponent for a fierce forehand drive or kill. Despite this, you should try and be positive about the shot when you do use it.

It is less dangerous if you attempt the volley nick with your opponent at the back, especially if you take the ball early. He or she will have to travel a long way to reach it, which will be tiring if it happens frequently, even if he does make an attacking shot. And of course, if you play your shot perfectly, you win the point.

The technique of the volleyed nick is a bit different from other volleys. Normally the volley is hit much like a basic drive, but if you are going for the nick then it is more like a karate chop, straight down, with quite a long follow-through directed to that small target. This makes it more accurate.

Sometimes it is better not to hit full blast. Slicing the ball may be preferable, and then it becomes something like a drop shot with the arm moving very quickly. This helps deceive the opponent, and also takes the pace of the ball so that even if it misses the nick, it has sufficient spin to stay short. Spin brings the ball down sharply.

Volleying can be related to mentality. A positive and perceptive mentality makes and takes initiatives. It seeks a purpose. There is a close analogy with boxing, in which the fighter is constantly jabbing away, and then suddenly takes his chance and flashes out the winning punch. With that attitude, and with the body and mind trained and balanced, you can win a rally.

Some players develop a skilful volley into the nick quite quickly and others don't. Some have a natural feeling for it and those who don't can achieve a similar facility by practising. It may take longer but, in any case, a lot of practice is necessary. With all the talent in the world you can't succeed without being adequately prepared.

To gain strength you must practise by yourself. Practise from the back, from the middle, down the wall. Then do cross-court practices from the middle, hitting the ball on to the front wall and then to the side wall, so that it comes back to you. After acquiring strength this way, practise for accuracy. For that you will need someone to feed you.

Take up a position as if you were playing a game. If you are on the 'T', the feeder can provide a ball for you to try to kill, followed by a different ball. Eventually you should have to deal with balls coming from every direction.

It is this sort of training that helped me to develop the Jahangir volley. Rahmat, himself a very good volleyer, reckons no one else has worked as hard on this. We spent hours together and it has become a very strong shot. But Jansher Khan has improved on this shot as well. He too has realized how crucial it can be. And if the lower 17-inch tin becomes a permanent feature of world squash, the volley will become even more important.

Some players have become good volleyers at squash because they were good at tennis, where the shot is essential. However there are important differences in the ways in which the volley should be played in the two games.

Because of the heavy racket, the volley in tennis requires strength in the body, the shoulder, or the whole of the arm. You stiffen the arm and push as, for instance, in shot-putting. But in squash it is more of an arm movement. On the forehand the volley can even be whipped, if need be. Generally speaking the follow-through on the volley is discouraged in tennis, whereas in squash it can be played like a drive, especially on low shots.

To do this you have to be balanced and in position. If you are out of position and off balance you will worsen the situation, and you won't be able to do much with the ball anyway.

46. *To hit the volley like a drive you need to be well positioned – as Rodney Martin is here for the forehand cross-court*

The ball must contact the middle of the racket, the arm has to be in a good position, and the follow-through must be correct.

There are plenty of good squash players who never learn this properly. Some of them use the volley mostly as a means of returning serve. Although some of them get away with it, they can usually only do so up to a certain level. The volley is a stroke that can save you a lot of hard labour and can make the difference between being a good player or an outstanding one.

8. The Short Game

47. Rodney Martin, master of the drop shot.

Rodney Martin, a uniquely brilliant talent, symbolises the greater creativity of the modern top-level game. World-class squash is now played much more to all four corners of the court, rather than principally to the back two, as used to be the case in the 1970s and early 80s. The Australian three times reached the final of the British Open – in 1988, 1989 and 1990 – first taking Jahangir to four games and then to five. He also beat Jansher Khan in the world team championships final of 1989. What made it very difficult for any player to contain him when he was firing on all cylinders was his ability to put the ball in the nick. Martin can do this with volleys and drop shots from almost any part of the court, but particularly on the backhand which he sometimes uses to slice the ball heavily. His match with Jahangir in the semi-final of the 1987 British Open, when he nearly won in straight games, is regarded as one of the most skilfully thrilling matches ever seen at Wembley

The Short Game

Gone are the days when a good player could manage without an effective short game. All the top players have learnt to be skilful in this area as well as to play a tight line and length. They have to be artists as well as artisans. With the developments in synthetic rackets and slower balls, an even greater premium has been placed on deceptive drops and boasts.

Brush them up regularly. There are useful exercises and instructions in our book *Winning Squash*, which good players, as well as beginners, would do well to follow. The routine of moving along the cut line, playing drops from all angles, backhand and forehand, into both nicks should be practised regularly. So should the routine with two players alternating drives with boasts or volley boasts, moving from the forehand side wall to the backhand side wall and back to the forehand side wall again.

At a high level it is important to have a good short game to keep the opponent 'honest' (i.e. to keep him guessing as to whether the ball is going short or long and thus to stop him 'cheating' by edging back from the 'T'). It is also vital to take advantage of an opponent's tiredness.

Deception is closely related to effectiveness in the front court. Most deceptive of all can be the straight drop from the back of the court, clinging to the side wall. It deceives because it is played from an area where drops are used less (and at lower standards of the game, hardly at all), and because it is hard to see whether the striker is going to drive the ball or drop it.

The value of the straight clinging drop from the back is that it can break up the game of an opponent who is either becoming too relentlessly attritional or too forcefully aggressive

with a driving game. Even if you don't play it quite right (for instance, if you play it a little too high), you will probably get away with it because a ball close to the side wall is hard to attack and still harder to kill. If the opponent is not expecting it, he or she may move late, too late to kill it. If tired, quite a moderate clinging drop may reveal that his (or her) alertness and speed are ebbing away.

The straight, clinging drop can be hit quite hard. Take the racket up high and twist the upper body as if to show for a drive, but then bring the racket down quite fast, thrusting the bottom edge of the face under the ball with slice. This gives more control and makes it hard to read the type of shot and the movement of the wrist. Transfer the weight forward as for a drive. If you do it right you will paralyse your opponent until after the ball has been hit, yet not make excessive demands of touch and feel upon yourself. If it's a winner, it can look like a wonderful shot, although actually it's not quite as difficult as it looks.

There is a practice routine which is used in the Khan camp quite a lot. It is called drop-drop, length-length. It enables you to improve two kinds of drop shot, at the front and the back, and two kinds of drive, from the front and the back. It goes as follows:

One player hits a straight backhand drop down the wall and stays back at the side of the

48. *Deceptive drops and boasts are at a premium in the modern game. Brett Martin has to try to guess which Jahangir is playing here. The racket can go inside or under the ball with this same preparation*

49. *A good short game can exploit an opponent's tiredness and prevent him from hanging back. Jahangir's famous backhand drop provides more work for Del Harris to do*

court. The other runs and plays a drop from the drop, again straight. Then the first player runs forward and hits a really hard deep length from the front which goes to the back wall. The second player runs to the back and takes the ball off the back wall, hitting a hard length down the wall; the first player then runs and plays the straight low drop, clinging to the wall if possible. This routine enables you to learn two shots from two very different positions.

Be careful with the straight drop from the back. You must strike it differently depending on whether the ball bounces on the floor first or hits the back wall first. If it hits the floor and then the back wall, the ball sits up. If it hits the back wall and then the floor, it tends to gather speed. It is also spinning differently. If the ball hits the back wall first, beware of dragging your drop shot down into the tin.

The same principle applies when the ball hits the side wall low down, before it hits the floor – it tends to shoot. You must then react more quickly and make more of an effort to get your racket under the ball. A ball that lands on the back wall is leaving your racket when you make the shot. This means you have to travel with it, get under it even more, and follow through more.

Although this may prove more difficult, it has its advantages. As you travel with the ball you can show as though you are hitting hard to a length. Then cut under the ball instead and it will go short and clinging. This deception is invaluable, especially as the ball can be hit quite hard. If it is played properly it is difficult to return, even if the opponent is well positioned. The wrist is hard to read when the racket moves as though making a drive.

People often suggest that a drop shot from the back is both difficult and dangerous. But if basic ball control is practised and developed, a good player can do almost whatever he or she wants. This shot is being used more and more. At the time of writing, a lower 17-inch tin is being employed at the top level of the game, which encourages drops from the back.

Use the drop shot when your opponent is

tired, and use it with variety. Watch for an opponent who is beginning to anticipate, and mix in another shot with the same preparation. For instance, if the ball is away from the side wall there is an option to play across court as well, especially on the forehand side. You can suddenly turn and play it cross-court, with the second bounce going somewhere near the side wall. Even if the opponent reaches it, it may still be difficult to cope with. There is a further variation: if the ball comes off the back wall back down the court, you can shape as if to play cross-court and instead pull the ball further across on to the opposite side wall – the reverse angle. The ball will return roughly in the direction from which it came.

Although we have picked out the straight drop as one of the most valuable shots of all, remember to practise the full short game repertoire. Often the trickle boast – played quickly on to the side wall and then the front wall from a short position – is a good option. Another variation is to shape to play a drop from a short central positon, but to cause it to strike the side wall close to the join with the front wall. This brings the ball out into the middle again and may wrongfoot an opponent who is rushing towards the front corner trying to anticipate.

Remember to practise the low sliced drop whose *second* (not first) bounce lands in the nick. It is often a winner. Shape as though to play a straight drop, dragging the opponent forward, but then delay and play it late, twisting the wrist so that the ball goes away across court. Even if the opponent changes direction, the ball will be leaving him, and he may not reach it before the second bounce at or near the side wall.

However you practise, try to be creative. Most players nowadays are good in the front court, and the trend at a high level is towards more inventive squash in all four corners of the court. So use your imagination. Try things. You might surprise yourself, as well as the opponent.

50. *Putting the bottom edge of the racket underneath the ball gives more control and makes it harder to read the exact movement of the wrist. Jahangir's forehand drop shot has kept Jansher from anticipating it until after it is played*

SECTION III – Planning the Future
9. Playing for Life

51. Stuart Sharp, fitter at forty.

Stuart Sharp is not a famous squash player, but he has a famous story. Once an overweight wealthy businessman, he spotted Jahangir as an unknown 15-year-old practising at Wembley. 'There was something special about him, a sort of aura, and I knew he was going to be a world champion,' said Sharp. Sharp predicted this would happen within a couple of years, which few thought possible at the time. So convinced was he, that he gave up everything to concentrate on making a film of how it happened. In the process a film about squash with religion in it became a religious film about squash; and eventually Sharp became converted to the Muslim faith. He also changed his attitude and his physique to become an active, fit person and a useful player. He did this even though he did not begin till he was well into his thirties. Now in his forties he keeps more active than he has ever done. The older player can find inspiration in this. It is quite possible to improve even at a later age, provided you concentrate on skills and gradually increase your physical output. A healthy regimen and the feelings of well-being it engenders can become the basis of a new life

Playing for Life

Squash is one of the top participatory sports in Britain, and looks like extending that reputation around the globe. One of the reasons is that you can start to play at any age. And you don't have to give up because you aren't as young or as good as you once were. It will help keep you young. You can play for life.

Squash is also part of a sports and leisure movement that is growing throughout the industrialized world. Why is that? What chords is it striking? Lost chords perhaps.

The philosophers have called it alienation; the psychologists point out that people are out of touch with their feelings about each other. To take part in a demanding physical exercise that gets the heart rate up and keeps it there, is healthy; to share such an activity with others is healing and therapeutic.

Sport is medically helpful, and it is psychologically invaluable too. It can help give purpose. Life sometimes lacks that.

Whether it is a clerk or a secretary lacking creativity, curiosity or control in their job; whether it is a salesman with a secret contempt for his product, for his customers who force him to put up a show in order to sell, and for his colleagues and rivals with whom he is in a competitive fight; whether it is a manager, who has to make so many decisions under pressure that the tension wells up inside like a thermometer's mercury; or whether it is a worker who is a tiny atom in the complicated monster of the factory – all need something to help them get away from the day-to-day and to integrate the personality.

Exercise can do that by bringing out something of your inner nature. You may feel the

system crushes you; you may feel condemned to live by the sweat of your brow; you may even feel like an enigmatic castaway on a lonely planet. But squash can help you transcend all this. It can help reveal that, in many senses, the kingdom of heaven is within you.

It is entirely untrue, therefore, that sport is all very well in its place, but that it is secondary to the 'important' things in life, such as politics or economics or culture. There is evidence to suggest that play is part of the basis of civilisation.

Play is found in most primitive societies, probably because a kind of play instinct can be instrumental in gaining knowledge. The universe is a giant puzzle from which answers have to be wrested, like an opponent who keeps his cards or shots close to his chest. A game pattern can perhaps be seen in the origins

52. *Use a good drop shot when you are older. Heather McKay, here seen beating Ann Smith on the way to the 1979 world title, was still the best in the world when she was nearly 40*

of poetry, literature, and the arts, which all have elaborate sets of rules. Play has elements of beauty, grace, rhythm, and harmony.

Play is free. It is the stepping outside of real life into a temporary world. It has an only pretend quality about it. Though play is an interlude, it becomes an integral part of life as a regularly recurring relaxation. Its real meaning lies in its ability to express what we feel.

Play creates order. To the confusion of life it brings a greater perfection. Deviation from the rules spoils the game, for when they are broken the play-world threatens to collapse. The referee's word breaks the magic spell and sets real life going again. The cheat or the spoilsport, by withdrawing from the game, robs it of its illusion. He ruins the magic world.

Leisure, play and sport are often a precondition of happiness and productivity. That suggests the potential squash has. It makes no sense at all to give it up just because you can't be as good as you once were, or because you have less time. You may be shortening your life as well as lessening the quality of it.

Even if you only play once a week, keep going. And even if you are afraid to start again, seek advice from a friend or a coach, and try. You can attain a remarkably high standard at a good age if you are careful, optimistic and patient. If you don't believe it, look around. There are plenty of examples.

Very often the belief that it is not possible to improve is the real barrier to doing so. The first thing is to look at technique rather than training. Technique can always be worked on, even if your body has days when it doesn't function at its best.

Start with the serve. This makes few physical demands and some improvement can usually be made in this department. With an effective serve it is sometimes possible to start in control of the rally. Nasrullah Khan once won 9-0, 9-0, 9-0 in the British Open because of his beautiful lob serve. Make it strike the side wall high in front of the receiver. If allowed to drop the ball should end up within two rackets' length of the backwall.

Try using the lob more in other areas of your game as well. Acquire a lob consistently to the corners and you will have developed plenty of ball control. The opponent won't often be able to do much with it. If you do produce a good lob and the opponent has to resort to a boast to return it, try to anticipate better where the ball will go. Then use a good drop shot. Up to a useful standard you can win many points by this combination of shots alone.

Practise the long distance drop shot. This requires little physical effort, and can further reduce physical effort by opening up the court and shortening the action. Concentrate on making the sort of shots that will put the opponent in difficulties, rather than preparing for long-drawn-out rallies.

You can often make openings with the second or third shot. Long distance drops can be played straight so that they cling to the wall. And a three-wall boast can be surprisingly effective. Practise this thoroughly. In time you should be able to make it hit two side walls.

Another ploy is to concentrate more on volleys. Advance one step and take the ball early and you can sometimes do a lot with it. If you hit a good serve the opponent will probably either play straight or boast. If he or she plays straight, try and get in to volley, and if the situation looks right, attempt to drop it into the nick. Watch the vintage players. Hashim Khan would not try to rally too much now. He serves, and the ball goes in the nick, and that's it.

There is no need for practice to be tiring. The shape of the court is such that by practising in the right way the ball will always come back to you. This will certainly happen with the three-wall boast. It should, too, with the cross-court drop shot. In this single-minded way, by developing a few really well-practised strokes to follow a clever service you can sometimes hold your own with younger, fitter players.

People used to say you should stop squash at 40. You should be careful if you are starting squash at 40. But if you are sensible, and build up any increase in activity gradually, you can play till a ripe old age. There are more and more

53. *Two golden oldies. Geoff Hunt was still tops at 34 years old; Hashim Khan was British Open champion at 42 and played to a high standard into his 70s*

Below left: 54. *As you get older stretching becomes more and more important. Glen Brumby, still a youngster at 30, shows how it is done*

veterans' and vintage events to help you do this.

If you find running difficult, try to walk as much as possible. Walking can be a useful build-up to jogging, and it is a far better exercise in itself than many people realize. Walking can get you quite a long way on a squash court. Two long steps cover a wide radius from the 'T'. With good anticipation you may not have to run, so make a conscious effort to prepare earlier, with good footwork and a high backswing to give you time to play the strokes.

As you get older the muscles can get a little weaker, and so stretching is important. To keep the muscles going they need to be well maintained. Lightweight training helps to keep the circulation going into them. Try an exercise like this one: take a very long step, maximum stretch, and then balance it. Don't let your hands touch the ground. Then move from side wall to side wall in this way. Afterwards, do gentle running. Running backwards is good for the back. Do it according to your ability. With lightweight training like this you will last longer. Stretching will help stave off injuries.

Warming-up exercises before you play become more and more important for the older

player. Warming-down is necessary too. Lie on the floor on your back. Then get up half way. Then lie straight and pull your muscles in, tensing the whole body, even the jaws, and slowly relax back.

It is vital not to stop playing for any length of time when you are older, or you will deteriorate quite quickly. It is therefore wise to think about how to keep your morale up. It is understandable for older players to feel depressed if they think their standard is going down. Try to get on a club league, even if it is a low division. It makes the squash more social, helps to occupy the mind, and any small achievement can give pleasure. Find opponents you enjoy playing.

Losing weight and playing better squash sometimes go together. It makes good sense to have a well-planned diet. Plenty has been written on how to achieve this, and our knowledge of how to eat healthily is at last becoming better communicated. Take notice of what informed sources say. It may benefit you more than you realize. With the correct fuel as well as correct maintenance of the body, you can keep your strength for a long time.

Remember that Hashim won the British Open at 42 years of age. Though this cannot be possible now, because of the greatly increased speed of the modern game, it is an example of the tremendous achievement attainable at a relatively late age. There will be plenty more who do great things at this age in the future. One must guard against the attitude that says: 'Oh, I'm 42 (or 52, or 62) now; I can't really do anything.'

Play at your own level in your own particular way and the rewards can be immense. It will help you to feel better. On really good days it can create a sense of oneness as a human being. It can help create experiences similar to those sought through yoga. Fatigue plus commitment plus passion can produce a perception of something real, of being part of something greater. Sportsmen and women occasionally have the feeling that they and the world, and their team-mates, and their opponents, are one.

Elements in sport are structurally similar to religion. There is a clear aim. There is a bounded situation, a kind of sacred space, an ordered nature. Marking out a containment, as in a court, enables us to let go of confusion. We know what the rules are, and we rely on this discipline. It frees us of the baggage of having to cope.

Because of the experiences of ecstasy and release that are possible, it could be that sport will increasingly be used to find out how to improve one's outlook on life. Yoga seeks to create experiences such as concentrated attention, effortless movement, and lack of judgement. The beauty is that many sportsmen and women of averagely good skills can achieve this, when previously it was thought that only those with religious predilections could do so.

Certainly sport can put you in touch with yourself in mind, body and spirit. There are many other ways, such as meditation, prayer, and psychotherapy, but sport can be one of them. Squash could be yours.

55. *Diet well and stay slim. With correct fuel and maintenance the body engine can go on a long time. Here Geoff Hunt, at 33, and Jonah Barrington, at 38, contest a British Open quarterfinal*